The Turkey Book

Quick and Easy:
101 Turkey and Chicken Rollups

Frankie Roe

The Turkey Book

For information contact: www.frankieroe.com
Photo Credit: Chyrelle "Cherry" Graham

ISBN: 978-0-6926080-8-1
First Edition: June 2020

Library of Congress Control Number (applied for)

TABLE OF CONTENTS

DEDICATION

This book is dedicated to anyone and everyone that has wanted a solution to becoming healthier and wanted an alternative for healthy snacking. It is my hope that the snacks listed in this book will bless your soul and inspire you to implement healthy eating habits in your daily food choices. Thank you for entrusting me with your health. Remember, your health is your wealth!

INTRODUCTION

Changing our eating habits can be a dreaded transformation. Learning what to eat, how much to eat, and how often to eat can be a worrisome burden. It doesn't make it any easier when new diets are popping up every day: South Beach Diet, Mediterranean Diet, Whole 30, Low-carb diets, juice diets...you name it and it is out there. Working in the health and fitness industry for eight years has afforded me the opportunity to see many different alternatives to becoming healthier and happier. I have seen people spend lots of time and money to get down to their desired size or weight. I have also seen many of these people put the weight right back on.

I, myself, have tried countless diets and multiple programs; none of them have worked for the long haul...and some have not worked at all. After all this time, what I have learned is that the drive to look good for a wedding or a special event is not what will help us to be successful. In my personal experience, it has been when I place my health above my vanity that I am able to succeed in not only achieving my goals but keeping weight off.

It is my belief that if you change the way you think, you can ultimately change the way you eat. This is the reason why I founded Frankie Roe Exhorting Enterprises. Our goal is to support, encourage, and provide guidance in the midst of uncertainty and a sea of fad diets and confusion.

At F.R.E.E, we believe that your health is your wealth and that the "Anti Inflammatory, Blood Type O, and Paleo" (AOP) lifestyle will help guide you there. AOP combines the best of the three dietary concepts that have worked for me and allowed me to sustain healthy eating habits. The result is a healthy, attainable, and sustainable dietary lifestyle.

The journey which led me to discover the first of these successful diets was a painful one. I had a herniated disk and was bound for neck surgery. The pain was excruciating, so I decided to be proactive about my health and investigate alternative medicine. I did hot yoga, visited a naturopath, and most importantly, I changed my diet. After five months on the Anti-inflammatory Diet and consciously putting my health first, I was able to cancel my surgery! The herniated disk had been reabsorbed into my body, and my neurosurgeon called me a walking miracle.

In 2003 I discovered a book by Dr. Peter D 'Adamo called Eat Right for Your Blood Type. In altering my diet to eat for my blood type, unwanted pounds were quickly shed, even from problem areas that thousands of dollars and countless hours of personal training sessions had failed to conquer. The Type O Diet gave me great results (I lost 10 pounds fast!), but it was a struggle for me to maintain as it was gluten-free and dairy-free, and I *love* bread and dairy. Therefore, I have made it just one part of the AOP program: integrating the best of what each of these diets has to offer while maintaining options.

To complete the trinity that is the AOP diet, we added in what some call "the oldest diet in the world" – Paleo. It is no secret that eating clean is good for you, and the Paleo diet is an excellent example of that. These three diets combined give us not only healthy choices, but variety in those choices. In my research I found the Paleo diet to be strict but doable. I have been able to use this diet to trim problem areas very quickly. Out of the trinity I would have to say that the Paleo diet would probably be my favorite. It is my favorite because it allows so much room for food creativity and that alone stimulates a certain part of my brain and makes me do the happy dance.

In this turkey roll book, you will find recipes that have aided me in reducing my weight and, more importantly, attaining good health. They have been instrumental in starting the AOP lifestyle for the past eight years and now I am happy to be sharing them with you. These lighthearted snacks will assist you on your road to healthy, living. We are all on a journey, and it is my hope that this book will be a significant part of yours. Enjoy the recipes you will find here and share them with your friends and family, so that they too can be on the journey of healthy living.

Cheers!

SUBSTITUTIONS

Use this "substitutions chart" to create the perfect chicken or turkey roll for you. Remember, the rolls are created with a certain taste in mind, but it is simply up to you to create your very own snack experience.

Exchange this....	For this...
Boar's Head Golden Classic Oven Roasted Chicken Breast 42% lower sodium for any meat in a recipe.	Boar's Head No Salt Added Turkey Breast, premium angus roast beef, or any other meat from this brand.
Boar's Head No Salt Added Turkey Breast for any meat in a recipe.	Golden Classic Oven Roasted Chicken Breast - 42% lower sodium, premium angus roast beef, or any other meat from this brand.
Apples- for any apple in a recipe.	Red delicious, gala, pink lady, golden delicious, honey crisp, granny smith, fuji, or any apple that you enjoy.
Bell Peppers- for any pepper in a recipe.	Green, yellow, red, orange or any pepper that you enjoy.
Berries- for any berry in a recipe.	Strawberries, raspberries, boysenberries, blueberries, or any berry that you enjoy.
Cherries- for any cherry in a recipe.	Rainier, bing, jubilee, selah, or any cherry that you enjoy.
Citrus Fruit- for any citrus fruit in a recipe.	Orange, grapefruit, lemon, lime, or any citrus fruit you enjoy.
Cucumber- for any cucumber style in a recipe.	Sweet, dill, half sour, or any pickle that you enjoy.

Grapes- for any grape in a recipe.	Red, black, green or any grape that you enjoy.
Leafy greens- for any leafy green in a recipe.	Collards, kale, bok choy, spring greens, spinach, or any leafy green you enjoy.
Lettuce- for any lettuce in a recipe.	Iceberg, romaine, butter head, arugula, chard, escarole, leaf lettuce, or any lettuce that you enjoy.
Olive- for any olive in a recipe.	Green, black, kalamata, cerignola, or any olive that you enjoy.
Nuts- for any nut in a recipe.	Almonds, pecans, walnuts, pine nuts, or any nuts that you enjoy.
Onion- for any onion in a recipe.	Red, yellow, Walla Walla sweet, white, green, leek, pearl, or any onion that you enjoy.
Plums- for any plum in a recipe.	Red, black, coe's golden drop, merryweather damson, or any plum that you enjoy.
Raisins- for any raisin in a recipe.	Golden raisins, sultanas, and currants or any raisin you enjoy.
Squash- for any squash in the squash family in a recipe.	Butternut, zucchini, spaghetti, acorn, pumpkin, delicata or any squash that you enjoy.

CHICKEN

CHICKEN, ALMONDS, AVOCADO & BUTTER LETTUCE

PREP: 10-15 MIN | COOK: N/A | SERVINGS: 2

INGREDIENTS:

2 slices of Golden Classic Oven Roasted Chicken Breast 42% lower sodium

Chopped or shredded butter lettuce

8-10 slices of almonds

2-4 slices of avocado

PREPARATION:

To assemble roll-ups: Place chicken on cutting board. Top with lettuce, almonds, and avocado.

Starting on one side, carefully roll-up chicken until chicken has been tightly rolled. Secure roll up with a wooden pick. Repeat with remaining ingredients.

CHICKEN, ALMONDS, BROCCOLI, GREEN ONIONS & RED GRAPES

PREP: 10-15 MIN | COOK: N/A | SERVINGS: 2

INGREDIENTS:

2 slices of Golden Classic Oven Roasted Chicken Breast 42% lower sodium

4-6 broccoli spears, raw or steamed, sliced

4-6 half slices of red grapes

2-4 green onions, chopped

8-10 slices of almonds

PREPARATION:

To assemble roll-ups: Place chicken on cutting board. Top with broccoli spears, red grapes, green onions, and almonds.

Starting on one side, carefully roll-up chicken until chicken has been tightly rolled. Secure roll up with a wooden pick. Repeat with remaining ingredients.

CHICKEN, ALMONDS, CARROTS & CHERRIES

PREP: 10-15 MIN | COOK: N/A | SERVINGS: 2

INGREDIENTS:

2 slices of Golden Classic Oven Roasted Chicken Breast 42% lower sodium

4-6 half slices of cherries

4-6 thin shredded or peeled carrots

4-6 slices of almonds

PREPARATION:

To assemble roll-ups: Place chicken on cutting board. Top with cherries, shredded or peeled carrots, and almond slices.

Starting on one side, carefully roll-up chicken until chicken has been tightly rolled. Secure roll up with a wooden pick. Repeat with remaining ingredients.

CHICKEN, ALMONDS, SPINACH & STRAWBERRY

PREP: 5-10 MIN | COOK: N/A | SERVINGS: 2

INGREDIENTS:

2 slices of olden Classic Oven Roasted Chicken Breast 42% lower sodium

8-10 leaves of spinach

6-8 slices of almonds

2-4 thin slices of strawberries

PREPARATION:

To assemble roll-ups: Place chicken on cutting board. Top with spinach leaves, almonds, and strawberries.

Starting on one side, carefully roll-up chicken until chicken has been tightly rolled. Secure roll up with a wooden pick. Repeat with remaining ingredients.

CHICKEN, APPLE (GRANNY SMITH) ARUGULA, & PECANS

PREP: 10-15 MIN | COOK: N/A | SERVINGS: 2

INGREDIENTS:

2 slices of Golden Classic Oven Roasted Chicken Breast 42% lower sodium

8-10 leaves of arugula,

4-6 slices of apple (granny smith), cut ¼ inch thick

8-10 slices of pecans (Trader Joes Sweet and Spicy)

PREPARATION:

To assemble roll-ups: Place chicken on cutting board. Top with arugula, pecans, and apples.

Starting on one side, carefully roll-up chicken until chicken has been tightly rolled. Secure roll up with a wooden pick. Repeat with remaining ingredients.

CHICKEN, APPLE, CARROTS & RED BELL PEPPERS

PREP: 10-15 MIN | COOK: N/A | SERVINGS: 2

INGREDIENTS:

2 slices of Golden Classic Oven Roasted Chicken Breast 42% lower sodium

4-6 slices of golden delicious apple (or your choice)

4-6 slices of sweet red bell pepper, ¼ inch thick

4-6 thin peeled or shredded carrots

PREPARATION:

To assemble roll-ups: Place chicken on cutting board. Top with apple slices, bell pepper, and carrots.

Starting on one side, carefully roll-up chicken until chicken has been tightly rolled. Secure roll up with a wooden pick. Repeat with remaining ingredient

CHICKEN, APPLE, CELERY, GREEN ONION & PECANS

PREP: 10-15 MIN | COOK: N/A | SERVINGS: 2

INGREDIENTS:

2 slices of Golden Classic Oven Roasted Chicken Breast 42% lower sodium

2-4 chopped green onion

4-6 slices golden delicious apple or your choice

4-5 sliced pecans

2-4 rectangle slices of celery

PREPARATION:

To assemble roll-ups: Place chicken on cutting board. Top with apple, pecans, green onions, and celery.

Starting on one side, carefully roll-up chicken until chicken has been tightly rolled. Secure roll up with a wooden pick. Repeat with remaining ingredients.

CHICKEN, APPLE, CRANBERRY & PEAR

PREP: 10-15 MIN | COOK: N/A | SERVINGS: 2

INGREDIENTS:

2 slices of Golden Classic
Oven Roasted Chicken
Breast 42% lower sodium
2-4 slices of pear
4-6 slices golden delicious
apple or your choice
6-8 fresh or dried
cranberries

PREPARATION:

To assemble roll-ups: Place
chicken on cutting board.
Top with apples,
cranberries, and pear slices.

Starting on one side,
carefully roll-up chicken
until chicken has been
tightly rolled. Secure roll up
with a wooden pick. Repeat
with remaining ingredients.

CHICKEN, APPLE, CRANBERRIES, PECANS & ONION

PREP: 10-15 MIN | COOK: N/A | SERVINGS: 2

INGREDIENTS:

2 slices of Golden Classic Oven Roasted Chicken Breast 42% lower sodium

4-6 slices golden delicious apple or your choice

4-6 slices of raw or roasted onion

6-8 fresh or dried cranberries

8-10 slices of pecans

PREPARATION:

To assemble roll-ups: Place chicken on cutting board. Top with apples, cranberries, pecans, and onion slices.

Starting on one side, carefully roll-up chicken until chicken has been tightly rolled. Secure roll up with a wooden pick. Repeat with remaining ingredients.

CHICKEN, APPLES, KIWI, PINEAPPLES & STRAWBERRIES

PREP: 10-15 MIN | COOK: N/A | SERVINGS: 2

INGREDIENTS:

2 slices of Golden Classic Oven Roasted Chicken Breast 42% lower sodium

4-6 slices golden delicious apple or your choice

2-4 slices of pineapple

2-4 slices of kiwi

2-4 thin slices of strawberries

PREPARATION:

To assemble roll-ups: Place chicken on cutting board. Top with apples, kiwi, strawberries, and pineapples.

Starting on one side, carefully roll-up chicken until chicken has been tightly rolled. Secure roll up with a wooden pick. Repeat with remaining ingredients.

CHICKEN, APPLES, PECANS & RAISINS

PREP: 10-15 MIN | COOK: N/A | SERVINGS: 2

INGREDIENTS:

2 slices of Golden Classic
Oven Roasted Chicken
Breast 42% lower sodium

2 slices of apples

4-5 sliced pecans

6-8 raisins

PREPARATION:

To assemble roll-ups: Place
chicken on cutting board.
Top with apples, raisins, and
pecans.

Starting on one side,
carefully roll-up chicken
until chicken has been
tightly rolled. Secure roll up
with a wooden pick. Repeat
with remaining ingredients.

CHICKEN, ARUGULA, CHERRY TOMATOES & PINE NUTS

PREP: 10-15 MIN | COOK: N/A MIN | SERVINGS: 2

INGREDIENTS:

2 slices of Golden Classic Oven Roasted Chicken Breast 42% lower sodium

8-10 leaves of arugula

4-6 half slices of cherry tomatoes

6-8 slices of pine nuts

PREPARATION:

To assemble roll-ups: Place chicken on cutting board. Top with arugula, pine nuts and cherry tomatoes.

Starting on one side, carefully roll-up chicken until chicken has been tightly rolled. Secure roll up with a wooden pick. Repeat with remaining ingredients.

CHICKEN, ARUGULA, MANDARIN & YELLOW BELL PEPPERS

INGREDIENTS:

2 slices of Golden Classic Oven Roasted Chicken Breast 42% lower sodium

8-10 leaves of arugula

4-6 slices of yellow bell peppers, ¼ inch thick

2-4 slices of mandarin (without rind)

PREPARATION:

To assemble roll-ups: Place chicken on cutting board. Top with arugula, mandarin, and bell peppers.

Starting on one side, carefully roll-up chicken until chicken has been tightly rolled. Secure roll up with a wooden pick. Repeat with remaining ingredients.

CHICKEN, ARUGULA, PEARS & WALNUT

PREP: 10-15 MIN | COOK: N/A | SERVINGS: 2

INGREDIENTS:

2 slices of Golden Classic
Oven Roasted Chicken
Breast 42% lower sodium

8-10 leaves of arugula

2-4 slices of pear

6-8 slices of walnuts

PREPARATION:

To assemble roll-ups: Place
chicken on cutting board.
Top with arugula, walnuts,
and pear.

Starting on one side,
carefully roll-up chicken
until chicken has been
tightly rolled. Secure roll up
with a wooden pick. Repeat
with remaining ingredients.

CHICKEN, ASPARAGUS, MUSHROOMS & TOMATO

PREP: 10-15 MIN | COOK: N/A | SERVINGS: 2

INGREDIENTS:

2 slices of Golden Classic Oven Roasted Chicken Breast 42% lower sodium

2-4 slices of asparagus

2-4 slices of mushrooms

2-4 slices of tomato

PREPARATION:

To assemble roll-ups: Place chicken on cutting board. Top with asparagus, mushrooms, and tomatoes.

Starting on one side, carefully roll-up chicken until chicken has been tightly rolled. Secure roll up with a wooden pick. Repeat with remaining ingredients.

CHICKEN, ASPARAGUS, RED ONION & YELLOW BELL PEPPER

PREP: 10-15 MIN | COOK: N/A | SERVINGS: 2

INGREDIENTS:

2 slices of Golden Classic Oven Roasted Chicken Breast 42% lower sodium

6-8 spears of asparagus

4-6 slices of yellow bell pepper, ¼ inch thick

4-6 slices of red onion, raw or roasted

PREPARATION:

To assemble roll-ups: Place chicken on cutting board. Top with asparagus, bell pepper, and red onion.

Starting on one side, carefully roll-up chicken until chicken has been tightly rolled. Secure roll up with a wooden pick. Repeat with remaining ingredients.

CHICKEN, AVOCADO, PINEAPPLE & RED BELL PEPPERS

PREP: 10-15 MIN   COOK: N/A   SERVINGS: 2

INGREDIENTS:

2 slices of Golden Classic
Oven Roasted Chicken
Breast 42% lower sodium

2-4 slices of pineapple

2-4 slices of avocado

4-6 slices of red bell
peppers, ¼ inch thick

PREPARATION:

To assemble roll-ups: Place
chicken on cutting board.
Top with pineapple,
avocado, and bell peppers.

Starting on one side,
carefully roll-up chicken
until chicken has been
tightly rolled. Secure roll up
with a wooden pick. Repeat
with remaining ingredients.

CHICKEN, BACON, LETTUCE & TOMATOES

PREP: 10-15 MIN | COOK: 15-20 MIN | SERVINGS: 2

INGREDIENTS:

2 slices of Golden Classic Oven Roasted Chicken Breast 42% lower sodium

Chopped or shredded lettuce

2 slices of bacon, drained

4 slices of tomato

PREPARATION:

Preheat oven to 375 degrees. Bake bacon in preheated oven until the bacon is deep golden-brown for 15 to 20 minutes or has desired crispness. Remove bacon from the baking sheet with tongs or a fork and drain on a paper towel-lined plate.

To assemble roll-ups: Place chicken on cutting board. Top with shredded lettuce, tomato slices, and 1 slice of bacon cut in half.

Starting on one side, carefully roll-up chicken until chicken has been tightly rolled. Secure roll up with a wooden pick. Repeat with remaining ingredients.

CHICKEN, BACON, ONION, PINEAPPLE & YELLOW BELL PEPPER

PREP: 10-15 MIN | COOK: 15-20 MIN | SERVINGS: 2

INGREDIENTS:

2 slices of Golden Classic Oven Roasted Chicken Breast 42% lower sodium

2 slices of bacon, drained

4-6 slices of yellow bell pepper, ¼ inch thick

4-6 slices of onion, raw or roasted

2-4 slices of pineapple

PREPARATION:

To assemble roll-ups: Place chicken on cutting board. Top with bell pepper, onion, pineapple, and 1 slice of bacon cut in half.

Starting on one side, carefully roll-up chicken until chicken has been tightly rolled. Secure roll up with a wooden pick. Repeat with remaining ingredients.

CHICKEN, BELL PEPPER, CUCUMBER & TOMATO

PREP: 10-15 MIN | COOK: N/A | SERVINGS: 2

INGREDIENTS:

2 slices of Golden Classic Oven Roasted Chicken Breast 42% lower sodium

4-6 slices of cucumber

4-6 slices of bell pepper, ¼ inch thick

4 slices of tomato

PREPARATION:

To assemble roll-ups: Place chicken on cutting board. Top with tomatoes, bell pepper, and cucumber.

Starting on one side, carefully roll-up chicken until chicken has been tightly rolled. Secure roll up with a wooden pick. Repeat with remaining ingredients.

CHICKEN, BELL PEPPER, GARLIC & SAUTÉED SPINACH

PREP: 10 MIN | COOK: 7-10 MIN | SERVINGS: 2

INGREDIENTS:

2 slices of Golden Classic Oven Roasted Chicken Breast 42% lower sodium

8-10 leaves of spinach

¼ clove garlic, minced

4-6 slices of bell pepper, ¼ inch thick

PREPARATION:

Heat the olive oil in a skillet over medium high heat. Add the garlic and sauté until fragrant. One minute after, add the spinach by the handful and toss with tongs until it wilts in 3 to 5 minutes. Season the spinach with salt and pepper. Let cool.

To assemble roll-ups: Place chicken on cutting board. Top with spinach and bell pepper mixture.

Starting on one side, carefully roll-up chicken until chicken has been tightly rolled. Secure roll up with a wooden pick. Repeat with remaining ingredients.

CHICKEN, BLUEBERRY, RASPBERRY, SPINACH & STRAWBERRY

PREP: 10-15 MIN | COOK: N/A | SERVINGS: 2

INGREDIENTS:

2 slices of Golden Classic Oven Roasted Chicken Breast 42% lower sodium

8-10 leaves of spinach

6-8 blueberries

6-8 raspberries

2-4 thin slices of strawberry

PREPARATION:

To assemble roll-ups: Place chicken on cutting board. Top with spinach, blueberries, raspberries, and strawberries.

Starting on one side, carefully roll-up chicken until chicken has been tightly rolled. Secure roll up with a wooden pick. Repeat with remaining ingredients.

CHICKEN, BLUEBERRIES, RED ONION & SPRING GREENS

PREP: 5-10 MIN | COOK: N/A | SERVINGS: 2

INGREDIENTS:

2 slices of Golden Classic Oven Roasted Chicken Breast 42% lower sodium

8-10 leaves of spring greens

6-8 blueberries

4-6 slices of red onions, raw or roasted

PREPARATION:

To assemble roll-ups: Place chicken on cutting board. Top with spring greens, blueberries, and red onions.

Starting on one side, carefully roll-up chicken until chicken has been tightly rolled. Secure roll up with a wooden pick. Repeat with remaining ingredients.

CHICKEN, BOK CHOY, BACON & ONION

PREP: 10 MIN | COOK: 15-20 MIN | SERVINGS: 2

INGREDIENTS:

2 slices of Golden Classic Oven Roasted Chicken Breast 42% lower sodium

Chopped leaves of bok choy

2 slices of bacon, drained

4-6 slices of onion, raw or roasted

PREPARATION:

Preheat oven to 375 degrees. Bake bacon in preheated oven until the bacon is deep golden-brown for 15 to 20 minutes or has desired crispness. Remove bacon from the baking sheet with tongs or a fork, and drain on a paper towel-lined plate

To assemble roll-ups: Place chicken on cutting board. Top with bok choy, onion, and bacon.

Starting on one side, carefully roll-up chicken until chicken has been tightly rolled. Secure roll up with a wooden pick. Repeat with remaining ingredients.

CHICKEN, BOK CHOY, BEETS & CARROTS

PREP: 10-15 MIN | COOK: N/A | SERVINGS: 2

INGREDIENTS:

2 slices of Golden Classic Oven Roasted Chicken Breast 42% lower sodium

Chopped leaves of bok choy

4-6 slices of beets

4-6 thin peeled or shredded carrots

PREPARATION:

To assemble roll-ups: Place chicken on cutting board. Top with bok choy, beets, and carrots.

Starting on one side, carefully roll-up chicken until chicken has been tightly rolled. Secure roll up with a wooden pick. Repeat with remaining ingredients.

CHICKEN, BOK CHOY, GINGER, ONION & RED BELL PEPPER

PREP: 10-15 MIN | COOK: N/A | SERVINGS: 2

INGREDIENTS:

2 slices of Golden Classic Oven Roasted Chicken Breast 42% lower sodium

Chopped leaves of bok choy

2-4 slices of ginger, dried or minced

4-6 slices of red bell pepper, ¼ inch thick

4-6 slices of onion, raw or roasted

PREPARATION:

To assemble roll-ups: Place chicken on cutting board. Top with bok choy, ginger, onion, and red bell pepper.

Starting on one side, carefully roll-up chicken until chicken has been tightly rolled. Secure roll up with a wooden pick. Repeat with remaining ingredients.

CHICKEN, BOK CHOY, GREEN ONIONS & TOASTED ALMONDS

PREP: 10-15 MIN | COOK: N/A | SERVINGS: 2

INGREDIENTS:

2 slices of Golden Classic Oven Roasted Chicken Breast 42% lower sodium

Chopped leaves of bok choy

4-6 slices of green onions, raw or roasted

8-10 slices of toasted almonds

PREPARATION:

To assemble roll-ups: Place chicken on cutting board. Top with bok choy, almonds, and green onions.

Starting on one side, carefully roll-up chicken until chicken has been tightly rolled. Secure roll up with a wooden pick. Repeat with remaining ingredients.

CHICKEN, BOYSENBERRIES, KIWI, STRAWBERRIES & SPINACH

PREP: 10-15 MIN | COOK: N/A | SERVINGS: 2

INGREDIENTS:

2 slices of Golden Classic
Oven Roasted Chicken
Breast 42% lower sodium

6-8 boysenberries

2-4 slices kiwi

2-4 thin slices of
strawberries

8-10 leaves of spinach

PREPARATION:

To assemble roll-ups: Place
chicken on cutting board.
Top with spinach,
boysenberries, strawberries,
and kiwi.

Starting on one side,
carefully roll-up chicken
until chicken has been
tightly rolled. Secure roll up
with a wooden pick. Repeat
with remaining ingredients.

CHICKEN, CARROTS, CHERRIES & CRANBERRIES

PREP: 10-15 MIN | COOK: N/A | SERVINGS: 2

INGREDIENTS:

2 slices of Golden Classic
Oven Roasted Chicken
Breast 42% lower sodium

4-6 thin peeled or shredded
carrots

4-6 half slices of cherries

6-8 cranberries, fresh or
dried

PREPARATION:

To assemble roll-ups: Place
chicken on cutting board.
Top with carrots, cherries,
and cranberries.

Starting on one side,
carefully roll-up chicken
until chicken has been
tightly rolled. Secure roll up
with a wooden pick. Repeat
with remaining ingredients.

CHICKEN, CARROTS, PLUMS & SPINACH

PREP: 10-15 MIN | COOK: N/A | SERVINGS: 2

INGREDIENTS:

2 slices of Golden Classic Oven Roasted Chicken Breast 42% lower sodium

2-4 slices of plums

4-6 thin peeled or shredded carrots

8-10 leaves of spinach

PREPARATION:

To assemble roll-ups: Place chicken on cutting board. Top with spinach, carrots, and plums.

Starting on one side, carefully roll-up chicken until chicken has been tightly rolled. Secure roll up with a wooden pick. Repeat with remaining ingredients.

CHICKEN, CARROTS, ROMAINE, RADISH & RED PEPPER

PREP: 10-15 MIN | COOK: N/A | SERVINGS: 2

INGREDIENTS:

2 slices of Golden Classic Oven Roasted Chicken Breast 42% lower sodium

Chopped or shredded romaine

4-6 slices of radish

4-6 thin peeled or shredded carrots

4-6 slices of red bell peppers, ¼ inch thick

PREPARATION:

To assemble roll-ups: Place chicken on cutting board. Top with shredded Romaine, radish, carrots, and bell peppers.

Starting on one side, carefully roll-up chicken until chicken has been tightly rolled. Secure roll up with a wooden pick. Repeat with remaining ingredients.

CHICKEN, CHERRIES (TART), CELERY & PECAN

PREP: 10-15 MIN | COOK: N/A | SERVINGS: 2

INGREDIENTS:

2 slices of Golden Classic Oven Roasted Chicken Breast 42% lower sodium

4-6 half slices of cherries (tart)

2-4 rectangle slices of celery

8-10 slices of pecans

PREPARATION:

To assemble roll-ups: Place chicken on cutting board. Top with cherries, celery, and pecans.

Starting on one side, carefully roll-up chicken until chicken has been tightly rolled. Secure roll up with a wooden pick. Repeat with remaining ingredients.

CHICKEN, CHERRIES, KALE & PLUM

PREP: 10-15 MIN | COOK: N/A | SERVINGS: 2

INGREDIENTS:

2 slices of Golden Classic Oven Roasted Chicken Breast 42% lower sodium

Chopped or shredded kale

4-6 half slices of cherries

2-4 slices of a plum

PREPARATION:

To assemble roll-ups: Place chicken on cutting board. Top with shredded kale, cherries, and plum.

Starting on one side, carefully roll-up chicken until chicken has been tightly rolled. Secure roll up with a wooden pick. Repeat with remaining ingredients.

CHICKEN, CHERRIES, ONION & SPINACH

PREP: 10-15 MIN | COOK: N/A | SERVINGS: 2

INGREDIENTS:

2 slices of Golden Classic Oven Roasted Chicken Breast 42% lower sodium

8-10 leaves of spinach

2-4 cherries, fresh or dried

4-6 slices of onion, raw or roasted

PREPARATION:

To assemble roll-ups: Place chicken on cutting board. Top with spinach, cherries, and onions.

Starting on one side, carefully roll-up chicken until chicken has been tightly rolled. Secure roll up with a wooden pick. Repeat with remaining ingredients.

CHICKEN, CRANBERRIES, NECTARINE & WALNUTS

PREP: 10-15 MIN | COOK: N/A | SERVINGS: 2

INGREDIENTS:

2 slices of Golden Classic Oven Roasted Chicken Breast 42% lower sodium

2-4 slices of nectarine

6-8 slices of walnuts

6-8 cranberries, fresh or dried

PREPARATION:

To assemble roll-ups: Place chicken on cutting board. Top with nectarine, walnuts, and cranberries.

Starting on one side, carefully roll-up chicken until chicken has been tightly rolled. Secure roll up with a wooden pick. Repeat with remaining ingredients.

CHICKEN, CUCUMBER, LIME & ONION

PREP: 10-15 MIN | COOK: N/A | SERVINGS: 2

INGREDIENTS:

2 slices of Golden Classic Oven Roasted Chicken Breast 42% lower sodium

4-6 slices of cucumber

4-6 slices of onion, raw or roasted

2-4 slices of lime (without rind)

PREPARATION:

Cut lime and squeeze lime juice on onion and cucumber. Cut two slices of the lime and peel off rind.

To assemble roll-ups: Place chicken on cutting board. Top with onion, lime slices and cucumber.

Starting on one side, carefully roll-up chicken until chicken has been tightly rolled. Secure roll up with a wooden pick. Repeat with remaining ingredients.

CHICKEN, CUCUMBER, OLIVES, RED ONIONS & TOMATOES

PREP: 10-15 MIN | COOK: N/A | SERVINGS: 2

INGREDIENTS:

2 slices of Golden Classic
Oven Roasted Chicken
Breast 42% lower sodium

4-6 half slices of olives

4 slices of tomatoes

4-6 slices of red onions, raw
or roasted

4-6 slices of cucumber

PREPARATION:

To assemble roll-ups: Place
chicken on cutting board.
Top with tomatoes, olives,
cucumbers, and red onions.

Starting on one side,
carefully roll-up chicken
until chicken has been
tightly rolled. Secure roll up
with a wooden pick. Repeat
with remaining ingredients.

CHICKEN, DRIED CRANBERRIES, KALE & YELLOW ONION

PREP: 10-15 MIN | COOK: N/A | SERVINGS: 2

INGREDIENTS:

2 slices of Golden Classic Oven Roasted Chicken Breast 42% lower sodium

Chopped or shredded kale

4-6 slices of yellow onion, raw or roasted

6-8 fresh or dried Cranberries

PREPARATION:

To assemble roll-ups: Place chicken on cutting board. Top with kale, cranberries, and onion slices.

Starting on one side, carefully roll-up chicken until chicken has been tightly rolled. Secure roll up with a wooden pick. Repeat with remaining ingredients.

CHICKEN, GREEN BELL PEPPERS, ONION & SPAGHETTI SQUASH

PREP: 10-15 MIN | COOK: 60 MIN | SERVINGS: 2

INGREDIENTS:

2 slices of Golden Classic Oven Roasted Chicken Breast 42% lower sodium

Cooled roasted spaghetti squash strands

4-6 slices of green bell peppers, ¼ inch thick

4-6 slices of onion, raw or roasted

PREPARATION:

Heat oven to 375 degrees. Brush the inside of each half of spaghetti squash with olive oil and sprinkle with coarse salt and freshly ground black pepper. Place cut sides up on a rimmed cookie sheet and put sheet into the oven. Bake for about 40 minutes, or until you can easily pierce the squash with a fork. Let cool for about 15 minutes, or until squash is cool enough to handle. With a fork, scrape out the spaghetti-like strands and prepare as desired.

To assemble roll-ups: Place chicken on cutting board. Top with 2 apples slices, 2-3 bell pepper slices, and carrots.

Starting on one side, carefully roll-up chicken until chicken has been tightly rolled. Secure roll up with a wooden pick. Repeat with remaining ingredients.

CHICKEN, JALAPEÑO (OPTIONAL), PAPAYA, RED BELL PEPPER & RED ONION

PREP: 10-15 MIN | COOK: N/A | SERVINGS: 2

INGREDIENTS:

2 slices of Golden Classic Oven Roasted Chicken Breast 42% lower sodium

2-4 slices of papaya

4-6 slices of red bell pepper, ¼ inch thick

4-6 slices of red onion, raw or roasted

2-4 thin slices of jalapeño (optional)

PREPARATION:

To assemble roll-ups: Place chicken on cutting board. Top with papaya, bell pepper, (jalapeno) and red onion.

Starting on one side, carefully roll-up chicken until chicken has been tightly rolled. Secure roll up with a wooden pick. Repeat with remaining ingredients.

CHICKEN, KIWI, NECTARINES & STRAWBERRY

PREP: 10-15 MIN | COOK: N/A | SERVINGS: 2

INGREDIENTS:

2 slices of Golden Classic Oven Roasted Chicken Breast 42% lower sodium

2-4 slices of nectarines

2-4 slices of kiwi

2-4 thin slices of strawberry

PREPARATION:

To assemble roll-ups: Place chicken on cutting board. Top with nectarines, kiwi, and strawberry.

Starting on one side, carefully roll-up chicken until chicken has been tightly rolled. Secure roll up with a wooden pick. Repeat with remaining ingredients.

CHICKEN, MANGO, PAPAYA & RED BELL PEPPER

PREP: 10-15 MIN | COOK: N/A | SERVINGS: 2

INGREDIENTS:

2 slices of Golden Classic Oven Roasted Chicken Breast 42% lower sodium

2-4 slices of mango

2-4 slices of papaya

4-6 slices of red bell pepper, ¼ inch thick

PREPARATION:

To assemble roll-ups: Place chicken on cutting board. Top with mango, papaya, and bell peppers.

Starting on one side, carefully roll-up chicken until chicken has been tightly rolled. Secure roll up with a wooden pick. Repeat with remaining ingredients.

CHICKEN, MUSHROOMS, SPAGHETTI SQUASH & TOMATOES

PREP: 10-15 MIN | COOK: 35-40 MIN | SERVINGS: 2

INGREDIENTS:

2 slices of Golden Classic Oven Roasted Chicken Breast 42% lower sodium

Cooled roasted spaghetti squash strands

4-6 thin sliced mushrooms

4 slices of tomatoes

PREPARATION:

Heat oven to 375 degrees. Brush the inside of each half of spaghetti squash with olive oil and sprinkle with coarse salt and freshly ground black pepper. Place cut sides up on a rimmed cookie sheet and put sheet into the oven. Bake for about 40 minutes, or until you can easily pierce the squash with a fork. Let cool for about 15 minutes, or until squash is cool enough to handle. With a fork, scrape out the spaghetti-like strands and prepare as desired.

To assemble roll-ups: Place chicken on cutting board.

Top with spaghetti squash strands, mushrooms, and tomatoes.

Starting on one side, carefully roll-up chicken

until chicken has been tightly rolled. Secure roll up with a wooden pick. Repeat with remaining ingredients.

CHICKEN, NECTARINE, ONION & TOMATO

INGREDIENTS:

2 slices of Golden Classic Oven Roasted Chicken Breast 42% lower sodium

4-6 slices of onion, raw or roasted

4 slices of tomato

2-4 slices of nectarine

PREPARATION:

To assemble roll-ups: Place chicken on cutting board. Top with onion, tomatoes, and nectarine.

Starting on one side, carefully roll-up chicken until chicken has been tightly rolled. Secure roll up with a wooden pick. Repeat with remaining ingredients.

CHICKEN, ONION, SQUASH & ZUCCHINI

PREP: 10-15 MIN | COOK: N/A | SERVINGS: 2

INGREDIENTS:

2 slices of Golden Classic Oven Roasted Chicken Breast 42% lower sodium

4-6 long rectangle-sliced squash

4-6 long rectangle-sliced zucchini

4-6 slices of onion, raw or roasted

PREPARATION:

To assemble roll-ups: Place chicken on cutting board. Top with squash, zucchini, and onions.

Starting on one side, carefully roll-up chicken until chicken has been tightly rolled. Secure roll up with a wooden pick. Repeat with remaining ingredients.

CHICKEN, PEPPERONCINI, RED ONION & SPINACH

PREP: 10-15 MIN | COOK: N/A | SERVINGS: 2

INGREDIENTS:

2 slices of Golden Classic Oven Roasted Chicken Breast 42% lower sodium

8-10 leaves of spinach

2-4 sliced pepperoncini

4-6 slices of red onion, raw or roasted

PREPARATION:

To assemble roll-ups: Place chicken on cutting board. Top with spinach, pepperoncini, and red onion.

Starting on one side, carefully roll-up chicken until chicken has been tightly rolled. Secure roll up with a wooden pick. Repeat with remaining ingredients.

CHICKEN, PINEAPPLE, SPINACH, YELLOW BELL PEPPERS

PREP: 10-15 MIN | COOK: N/A | SERVINGS: 2

INGREDIENTS:

2 slices of Golden Classic Oven Roasted Chicken Breast 42% lower sodium

2-4 slices of pineapple

8-10 leaves of spinach

4-6 slices of yellow bell peppers, ¼ inch thick

PREPARATION:

To assemble roll-ups: Place chicken on cutting board. Top with pineapple, spinach, and bell peppers.

Starting on one side, carefully roll-up chicken until chicken has been tightly rolled. Secure roll up with a wooden pick. Repeat with remaining ingredients.

CHICKEN, PINEAPPLE & ZUCCHINI

PREP: 10-15 MIN | COOK: N/A | SERVINGS: 2

INGREDIENTS:

2 slices of Golden Classic Oven Roasted Chicken Breast 42% lower sodium

4-6 long rectangle-sliced zucchini

2-4 slices of pineapple

PREPARATION:

To assemble roll-ups: Place chicken on cutting board. Top with zucchini and pineapple

Starting on one side, carefully roll-up chicken until chicken has been tightly rolled. Secure roll up with a wooden pick. Repeat with remaining ingredients.

CHICKEN, PUMPKIN & SAUTÉED KALE

PREP: 10-15 MIN | COOK: 30-35 MIN | SERVINGS: 2

INGREDIENTS:

2 slices of Golden Classic Oven Roasted Chicken Breast 42% lower sodium

Chopped or shredded of sautéed kale

2-4 cooled slices of pumpkin

PREPARATION:

Roasted pumpkin:
Preheat oven to 450 degrees. Cut and place pumpkin on parchment paper. Roast until pumpkin is tender, 30 to 35 minutes, tossing once and rotating sheets halfway through. Optional to add olive oil. (1 Tbsp) Allow to cool.

To assemble roll-ups: Place chicken on cutting board. Top pumpkin and kale.

Starting on one side, carefully roll-up chicken until chicken has been tightly rolled. Secure roll up with a wooden pick. Repeat with remaining ingredients.

CHICKEN, RED BELL PEPPERS & SAUTÉED COLLARDS

PREP: 10-15 MIN | COOK: N/A | SERVINGS: 2

INGREDIENTS:

2 slices of Golden Classic Oven Roasted Chicken Breast 42% lower sodium

6-8 leaves of sautéed collards

4-6 slices of red bell peppers, ¼ inch thick

PREPARATION:

To assemble roll-ups: Place chicken on cutting board. Top with collards and bell pepper.

Starting on one side, carefully roll-up chicken until chicken has been tightly rolled. Secure roll up with a wooden pick. Repeat with remaining ingredients.

CHICKEN, RED LETTUCE & RADISH

PREP: 5-10 MIN | COOK: N/A | SERVINGS: 2

INGREDIENTS:

2 slices of Golden Classic Oven Roasted Chicken Breast 42% lower sodium

Chopped or shredded red lettuce

4-6 slices of radish

Few leaves of cilantro

PREPARATION:

To assemble roll-ups: Place chicken on cutting board. Top with chopped lettuce, 2 radish slices, and cilantro leaves.

Starting on one side, carefully roll-up chicken until chicken has been tightly rolled. Secure roll up with a wooden pick. Repeat with remaining ingredients.

CHICKEN & ROASTED SWEET POTATO

PREP: 10 MIN | COOK: 35-45 MIN | SERVINGS: 2

INGREDIENTS:

2 slices of Golden Classic
Oven Roasted Chicken
Breast 42% lower sodium

2-4 sweet potatoes, cut into
long, thin rectangles

PREPARATION:

Preheat oven to 375. Lay
sweet potato on a cookie
sheet. Drizzle with olive oil
and season with salt and
pepper. Roast for 40
minutes or until soft.
Remove from oven and cool
off.

To assemble roll-ups: Place
chicken on cutting board.
Top with potatoes.

Starting on one side,
carefully roll-up chicken
until chicken has been
tightly rolled. Secure roll up
with a wooden pick. Repeat
with remaining ingredients.

CHICKEN, ROASTED SWEET POTATO, RED BELL PEPPER & YELLOW

PREP: 10-15 MIN | COOK: 40 MIN | SERVINGS: 2

INGREDIENTS:

2 slices of Golden Classic Oven Roasted Chicken Breast 42% lower sodium

2-4 sweet potatoes, cut into long, thin rectangles

4-6 slices yellow bell pepper, ¼ inch thick

4-6 slices red bell pepper, ¼ inch thick

PREPARATION:

Preheat oven to 375. Lay sweet potato on a cookie sheet. Drizzle with olive oil and season with salt and pepper. Roast for 40 minutes or until soft. Remove from oven and cool off.

To assemble roll-ups: Place chicken on cutting board. Top with sweet potato rectangles, and red and yellow bell peppers.

Starting on one side, carefully roll-up chicken until chicken has been tightly rolled. Secure roll up with a wooden pick. Repeat with remaining ingredients.

CHICKEN, SQUASH, YELLOW BELL PEPPERS & ZUCCHINI

PREP: 10 MIN | COOK: N/A | SERVINGS: 2

INGREDIENTS:

2 slices of Golden Classic Oven Roasted Chicken Breast 42% lower sodium

4-6 long rectangle-sliced zucchini

4-6 long rectangle-sliced squash

4-6 slices of yellow bell peppers, ¼ inch thick

PREPARATION:

To assemble roll-ups: Place chicken on cutting board. Top with zucchini, squash, and yellow bell peppers.

Starting on one side, carefully roll-up chicken until chicken has been tightly rolled. Secure roll up with a wooden pick. Repeat with remaining ingredients.

CHICKEN & STEAMED ASPARAGUS

PREP: 6-10 MIN | COOK: 10-15 MIN | SERVINGS: 2

INGREDIENTS:

2 slices of Golden Classic Oven Roasted Chicken Breast 42% lower sodium

6-8 asparagus spears

PREPARATION:

Wash asparagus. Cut off ends and steam until stem are cooked but still firm.

To assemble roll-ups: Place chicken on cutting board. Top with asparagus spears.

Starting on one side, carefully roll-up chicken until chicken has been tightly rolled. Secure roll up with a wooden pick. Repeat with remaining ingredients.

CHICKEN, SUN-DRIED TOMATOES & ZUCCHINI

PREP: 10-15 MIN   COOK: N/A   SERVINGS: 2

INGREDIENTS:

2 slices of Golden Classic Oven Roasted Chicken Breast 42% lower sodium

2-4 slices of sun-dried tomatoes

4-6 long rectangle-sliced zucchini

PREPARATION:

To assemble roll-ups: Place chicken on cutting board. Top with sun-dried tomatoes and zucchini.

Starting on one side, carefully roll-up chicken until chicken has been tightly rolled. Secure roll up with a wooden pick. Repeat with remaining ingredients.

TURKEY

TURKEY, ACORN SQUASH & APPLES

PREP: 10-15 MIN   COOK: 25-30 MIN   SERVINGS: 2

INGREDIENTS:

2 slices of Boar's Head No Salt Added Turkey Breast

2-4 slices of cooled acorn squash

4-6 slices of apples, golden delicious or your choice

PREPARATION:

Preheat oven to 400 degrees F. Cut and toss squash slices with olive oil, salt, and pepper together in a bowl until the squash is evenly coated; spread into a jelly roll pan. Roast in preheated oven until golden brown and tender, 25 to 30 minutes.

To assemble roll-ups: Place turkey on cutting board. Top with acorn squash and apples.

Starting on one side, carefully roll-up turkey until turkey has been tightly rolled. Secure roll up with a wooden pick. Repeat with remaining ingredients.

TURKEY, ALMONDS, APPLE & SPINACH

INGREDIENTS:

2 slices of Boar's Head No Salt Added Turkey Breast

4-6 slices of apples, golden delicious or your choice

8-10 slices of almonds

8-10 leaves of spinach

PREPARATION:

To assemble roll-ups: Place turkey on cutting board. Top with spinach, almonds, and apples.

Starting on one side, carefully roll-up turkey until turkey has been tightly rolled. Secure roll up with a wooden pick. Repeat with remaining ingredients.

TURKEY, ALMOND, BLUEBERRIES & KALE

PREP: 10-15 MIN | COOK: N/A | SERVINGS: 2

INGREDIENTS:

2 Slices of Boar's Head No Salt Added Turkey Breast

Chopped or shredded kale

6-8 blueberries

8-10 slices of almonds

PREPARATION:

To assemble roll-ups: Place turkey on cutting board. Top with kale, almonds, and blueberries.

Starting on one side, carefully roll-up turkey until turkey has been tightly rolled. Secure roll up with a wooden pick. Repeat with remaining ingredients.

TURKEY, APPLE & CRANBERRY

PREP: 10-15 MIN | COOK: N/A | SERVINGS: 2

INGREDIENTS:

2 slices of Boar's Head No
Salt Added Turkey Breast

4-6 slices of apple, golden
delicious or your choice

6-8 fresh or dried
cranberries

PREPARATION:

To assemble roll-ups: Place
turkey on cutting board. Top
with apples and cranberries.

Starting on one side,
carefully roll-up turkey until
turkey has been tightly
rolled. Secure roll up with a
wooden pick. Repeat with
remaining ingredients.

TURKEY, ARUGULA, AVOCADO & GRAPEFRUIT

PREP: 10-15 MIN | COOK: N/A | SERVINGS: 2

INGREDIENTS:

2 slices of Boar's Head No Salt Added Turkey Breast

8-10 leaves of arugula

2-4 slices of grapefruit (without rind)

2-4 slices of avocado

PREPARATION:

To assemble roll-ups: Place turkey on cutting board. Top with arugula, grapefruit, and avocado.

Starting on one side, carefully roll-up turkey until turkey has been tightly rolled. Secure roll up with a wooden pick. Repeat with remaining ingredients.

TURKEY, ARUGULA, FIGS & SHREDDED CARROTS

PREP: 10-15 MIN | COOK: N/A |SERVINGS: 2

INGREDIENTS:

2 slices of Boar's Head No Salt Added Turkey Breast

8-10 leaves of arugula

2-4 fresh or dried figs

4-6 thin peeled or shredded carrots

PREPARATION:

To assemble roll-ups: Place turkey on cutting board. Top with arugula, figs, and carrots.

Starting on one side, carefully roll-up turkey until turkey has been tightly rolled. Secure roll up with a wooden pick. Repeat with remaining ingredients.

TURKEY, ARUGULA, MUSHROOMS & RED BELL PEPPERS

PREP: 10-15 MIN | COOK: N/A | SERVINGS: 2

INGREDIENTS:

2 slices of Boar's Head No Salt Added Turkey Breast

8-10 leaves of arugula

4-6 thin sliced mushrooms

4-6 slices of red bell peppers, ¼ inch thick

PREPARATION:

To assemble roll-ups: Place turkey on cutting board. Top with arugula, mushrooms, and bell peppers.

Starting on one side, carefully roll-up turkey until turkey has been tightly rolled. Secure roll up with a wooden pick. Repeat with remaining ingredients.

TURKEY, ARUGULA, RED ONION & WATERMELON

PREP: 10-15 MIN | COOK: N/A | SERVINGS: 2

INGREDIENTS:

2 slices of Boar's Head No Salt Added Turkey Breast

8-10 leaves of arugula

2-4 slices of watermelon

4-6 slices of red onion, raw or roasted

PREPARATION:

To assemble roll-ups: Place turkey on cutting board. Top with arugula, watermelon, and onions.

Starting on one side, carefully roll-up turkey until turkey has been tightly rolled. Secure roll up with a wooden pick. Repeat with remaining ingredients.

TURKEY, ASPARAGUS, GINGER, GARLIC, RED BELL PEPPER & ONION

PREP: 10-15 MIN | COOK: N/A | SERVINGS: 2

INGREDIENTS:

2 slices of Boar's Head No Salt Added Turkey Breast

6-8 spears of asparagus

4-6 slices of red bell pepper, ¼ inch thick

4-6 slices of onion, raw or roasted

2-4 slices of ginger, dried or minced

¼ clove of garlic, minced

PREPARATION:

To assemble roll-ups: Place turkey on cutting board. Top with asparagus, bell peppers, onions, ginger, and garlic.

Starting on one side, carefully roll-up turkey until turkey has been tightly rolled. Secure roll up with a wooden pick. Repeat with remaining ingredients.

TURKEY, ASPARAGUS, SPINACH & SLICED ONION

INGREDIENTS:

2 slices of Boar's Head No Salt Added Turkey Breast

6-8 spears of asparagus

8- 10 leaves of spinach

4-6 slices of onion, raw or roasted

PREPARATION:

To assemble roll-ups: Place turkey on cutting board. Top with asparagus, spinach, and onions.

Starting on one side, carefully roll-up turkey until turkey has been tightly rolled. Secure roll up with a wooden pick. Repeat with remaining ingredients.

TURKEY, AVOCADO, NECTARINE & RED BELL PEPPER

PREP: 10-15 MIN | COOK: N/A | SERVINGS: 2

INGREDIENTS:

2 slices of Boar's Head No Salt Added Turkey Breast

2-4 slices of nectarine

2-4 slices of avocado

4-6 slices of red bell pepper, ¼ inch thick

PREPARATION:

To assemble roll-ups: Place turkey on cutting board. Top with nectarine, avocado, and bell pepper.

Starting on one side, carefully roll-up turkey until turkey has been tightly rolled. Secure roll up with a wooden pick. Repeat with remaining ingredients.

TURKEY, AVOCADO, MUSHROOM & SPINACH

PREP: 10-15 MIN | COOK: N/A | SERVINGS: 2

INGREDIENTS:

2 slices of Boar's Head No Salt Added Turkey Breast

2-4 slices of avocado

8- 10 leaves of spinach

4-6 thin sliced mushroom

PREPARATION:

To assemble roll-ups: Place turkey on cutting board. Top with spinach, mushrooms, and avocado.

Starting on one side, carefully roll-up turkey until turkey has been tightly rolled. Secure roll up with a wooden pick. Repeat with remaining ingredients.

TURKEY, BLUEBERRY, CHERRY, STRAWBERRY & SPINACH

PREP: 10-15 MIN | COOK: N/A | SERVINGS: 2

INGREDIENTS:

2 slices of Boar's Head No Salt Added Turkey Breast

8-10 leaves of spinach

4-6 half slices of cherries

2-4 thin slices of strawberry

6-8 blueberries

PREPARATION:

To assemble roll-ups: Place turkey on cutting board. Top with spinach, blueberries, strawberries, and cherries.

Starting on one side, carefully roll-up turkey until turkey has been tightly rolled. Secure roll up with a wooden pick. Repeat with remaining ingredients.

TURKEY, BOK CHOY, CARROTS & STEAMED GREEN BEANS

PREP: 10 MIN | COOK: 5-7 MIN | SERVINGS: 2

INGREDIENTS:

2 slices of Boar's Head No Salt Added Turkey Breast

Chopped leaves of bok choy

4-6 thin peeled or shredded carrots

4-6 steamed green beans

PREPARATION:

Place green beans in a medium saucepan. Bring to a boil, and steam to your desired degree of tenderness, for about 5 minutes. Once the beans have cooked, transfer them to a serving bowl. Toss with olive oil, garlic, salt, and pepper.

To assemble roll-ups: Place turkey on cutting board. Top with bok choy, carrots, and green beans.

Starting on one side, carefully roll-up turkey until turkey has been tightly rolled. Secure roll up with a wooden pick. Repeat with remaining ingredients.

TURKEY, BROCCOLI, CARROTS, RED BELL PEPPERS & SNOW PEAS

PREP: 10-15 MIN | COOK: N/A | SERVINGS: 2

INGREDIENTS:

2 slices of Boar's Head No Salt Added Turkey Breast

4-6 broccoli spears, raw or steamed

4-6 snow peas

4-6 thin peeled or shredded carrots

4-6 slices of red bell peppers, ¼ inch thick

PREPARATION:

To assemble roll-ups: Place turkey on cutting board. Top with broccoli, snow peas, carrots, and bell peppers.

Starting on one side, carefully roll-up turkey until turkey has been tightly rolled. Secure roll up with a wooden pick. Repeat with remaining ingredients.

TURKEY, BROCCOLI, RAISIN & RED ONION

PREP: 10-15 MIN | COOK: N/A | SERVINGS: 2

INGREDIENTS:

2 slices of Boar's Head No Salt Added Turkey Breast

4-6 broccoli spears, raw or steamed

6-8 raisins

4-6 slices of red onion, raw or roasted

PREPARATION:

To assemble roll-ups: Place turkey on cutting board. Top with broccoli, raisins, and onions.

Starting on one side, carefully roll-up turkey until turkey has been tightly rolled. Secure roll up with a wooden pick. Repeat with remaining ingredients.

TURKEY, BROCCOLI & ZUCCHINI

PREP: 10-15 MIN | COOK: N/A | SERVINGS: 2

INGREDIENTS:

2 slices of Boar's Head No Salt Added Turkey Breast

4-6 spears broccoli, raw or steamed

4-6 long rectangle-sliced zucchini

PREPARATION:

To assemble roll-ups: Place turkey on cutting board. Top with broccoli and zucchini.

Starting on one side, carefully roll-up turkey until turkey has been tightly rolled. Secure roll up with a wooden pick. Repeat with remaining ingredients.

TURKEY, CARROTS, CELERY & ONION

PREP: 10-15 MIN | COOK: N/A | SERVINGS: 2

INGREDIENTS:

2 slices of Boar's Head No Salt Added Turkey Breast

2-4 rectangle slices of celery

4-6 thin peeled or shredded carrots

2-4 slices of onion, raw or roasted

PREPARATION:

To assemble roll-ups: Place turkey on cutting board. Top with celery, carrots, and onion.

Starting on one side, carefully roll-up turkey until turkey has been tightly rolled. Secure roll up with a wooden pick. Repeat with remaining ingredients.

TURKEY, CARROTS, CUCUMBER & SPINACH

PREP: 10-15 MIN | COOK: N/A | SERVINGS: 2

INGREDIENTS:

2 slices of Boar's Head No Salt Added Turkey Breast

4-6 thin peeled or shredded carrots

8-10 leaves of spinach

4-6 slices of cucumber

PREPARATION:

To assemble roll-ups: Place turkey on cutting board. Top with spinach, cucumber, and carrots.

Starting on one side, carefully roll-up turkey until turkey has been tightly rolled. Secure roll up with a wooden pick. Repeat with remaining ingredients.

TURKEY, CARROTS, GREEN BELL PEPPERS & PINEAPPLE

PREP: 10-15 MIN | COOK: N/A | SERVINGS: 2

INGREDIENTS:

2 slices of Boar's Head No Salt Added Turkey Breast

2-4 slices of pineapple

4-6 thin peeled or shredded carrots

4-6 slices of green bell peppers, ¼ inch thick

PREPARATION:

To assemble roll-ups: Place turkey on cutting board. Top with carrots, bell peppers, and pineapples.

Starting on one side, carefully roll-up turkey until turkey has been tightly rolled. Secure roll up with a wooden pick. Repeat with remaining ingredients.

TURKEY, CARROTS, GREEN ONION, GRANNY SMITH & RED BELL

PREP: 10-15 MIN | COOK: N/A | SERVINGS: 2

INGREDIENTS:

2 slices of Boar's Head No Salt Added Turkey Breast

4-6 slices of granny smith apples

4-6 thin sliced or shredded carrots

4-6 red bell peppers, ¼ inch thick

2-4 chopped green onions

PREPARATION:

To assemble roll-ups: Place turkey on cutting board. Top with apples, green onions, bell peppers and carrots.

Starting on one side, carefully roll-up turkey until turkey has been tightly rolled. Secure roll up with a wooden pick. Repeat with remaining ingredients.

TURKEY, CARROTS, ONION & PARSNIPS

PREP: 10-15 MIN | COOK: N/A | SERVINGS: 2

INGREDIENTS:

2 slices of Boar's Head No Salt Added Turkey Breast

2-4 slices of parsnips

4-6 thin sliced or shredded carrots

4-6 slices of red onions, raw or roasted

PREPARATION:

To assemble roll-ups: Place turkey on cutting board. Top with parsnips, carrots, and onions.

Starting on one side, carefully roll-up turkey until turkey has been tightly rolled. Secure roll up with a wooden pick. Repeat with remaining ingredients.

TURKEY, CARROTS, RED BELL PEPPERS & ZUCCHINI

PREP: 10-15 MIN | COOK: N/A | SERVINGS: 2

INGREDIENTS:

2 slices of Boar's Head No Salt Added Turkey Breast

4-6 thin sliced or shredded carrots

4-6 long rectangle-sliced zucchini

4-6 red bell peppers, ¼ inch thick

PREPARATION:

To assemble roll-ups: Place turkey on cutting board. Top with zucchini, carrots, and bell peppers.

Starting on one side, carefully roll-up turkey until turkey has been tightly rolled. Secure roll up with a wooden pick. Repeat with remaining ingredients.

TURKEY, CARROTS, SQUASH & ZUCCHINI

PREP: 10-15 MIN | COOK: N/A | SERVINGS: 2

INGREDIENTS:

2 slices of Boar's Head No Salt Added Turkey Breast

4-6 thin sliced or shredded carrots

4-6 long rectangle-sliced zucchini

4-6 long rectangle-sliced squash

PREPARATION:

To assemble roll-ups: Place turkey on cutting board. Top with zucchini and squash.

Starting on one side, carefully roll-up turkey until turkey has been tightly rolled. Secure roll up with a wooden pick. Repeat with remaining ingredients.

TURKEY, CRANBERRIES, ONION & ROMAINE

PREP: 10-15 MIN | COOK: N/A | SERVINGS: 2

INGREDIENTS:

2 slices of Boar's Head No
Salt Added Turkey Breast

4-6 slices of onion, raw or
roasted

Chopped or shredded
romaine

6-8 fresh or dried
cranberries

PREPARATION:

To assemble roll-ups: Place
turkey on cutting board. Top
with romaine, cranberries,
and onion.

Starting on one side,
carefully roll-up turkey until
turkey has been tightly
rolled. Secure roll up with a
wooden pick. Repeat with
remaining ingredients.

TURKEY, CRANBERRIES, RED ONION & SPINACH

PREP: 10-15 MIN | COOK: N/A | SERVINGS: 2

INGREDIENTS:

2 slices of Boar's Head No Salt Added Turkey Breast

8-10 leaves of spinach

4-6 slices of red onion, raw or roasted

6-8 fresh or dried cranberries

PREPARATION:

To assemble roll-ups: Place turkey on cutting board. Top with spinach, cranberries, and onions.

Starting on one side, carefully roll-up turkey until turkey has been tightly rolled. Secure roll up with a wooden pick. Repeat with remaining ingredients.

TURKEY, CUCUMBER, GREEN BELL PEPPER & MANGO

PREP: 10-15 MIN | COOK: N/A | SERVINGS: 2

INGREDIENTS:

2 slices of Boar's Head No Salt Added Turkey Breast

4-6 slices of cucumber

2-4 slices of mango

4-6 slices of green bell pepper, ¼ inch thick

PREPARATION:

To assemble roll-ups: Place turkey on cutting board. Top with mango, cucumber, and bell pepper.

Starting on one side, carefully roll-up turkey until turkey has been tightly rolled. Secure roll up with a wooden pick. Repeat with remaining ingredients.

TURKEY, CUCUMBER, PAPAYA & TOMATO

PREP: 10-15 MIN | COOK: N/A | SERVINGS: 2

INGREDIENTS:

2 slices of Boar's Head No Salt Added Turkey Breast

4 slices of tomato

4-6 slices of cucumber

2-4 slices of papaya

PREPARATION:

To assemble roll-ups: Place turkey on cutting board. Top with papaya, cucumber, and tomato.

Starting on one side, carefully roll-up turkey until turkey has been tightly rolled. Secure roll up with a wooden pick. Repeat with remaining ingredients.

TURKEY, CUCUMBER, RED ONION & TOMATO

PREP: 10-15 MIN | COOK: N/A | SERVINGS: 2

INGREDIENTS:

2 slices of Boar's Head No Salt Added Turkey Breast

4 slices of tomato

4-6 slices of cucumber

4-6 slices of red onion, raw or roasted

PREPARATION:

To assemble roll-ups: Place turkey on cutting board. Top with tomato, cucumbers, and red onions.

Starting on one side, carefully roll-up turkey until turkey has been tightly rolled. Secure roll up with a wooden pick. Repeat with remaining ingredients.

TURKEY, CUCUMBER, SPINACH & TOMATO

PREP: 10-15 MIN | COOK: N/A | SERVINGS: 2

INGREDIENTS:

2 slices of Boar's Head No Salt Added Turkey Breast

8- 10 leaves of spinach

4-6 slices cucumber

4 slices of tomato

PREPARATION:

To assemble roll-ups: Place turkey on cutting board. Top with spinach, cucumber, and tomatoes.

Starting on one side, carefully roll-up turkey until turkey has been tightly rolled. Secure roll up with a wooden pick. Repeat with remaining ingredients.

TURKEY, CUCUMBER, TOMATO & YELLOW BELL PEPPER

PREP: 10-15 MIN | COOK: N/A | SERVINGS: 2

INGREDIENTS:

2 slices of Boar's Head No Salt Added Turkey Breast

4 slices of tomato

4-6 slices of cucumber

4-6 slices of yellow bell pepper, ¼ inch thick

PREPARATION:

To assemble roll-ups: Place turkey on cutting board. Top with tomato, cucumber, and bell peppers.

Starting on one side, carefully roll-up turkey until turkey has been tightly rolled. Secure roll up with a wooden pick. Repeat with remaining ingredients.

TURKEY, GRAPES, KALE & WALNUTS

PREP: 10-15 MIN | COOK: N/A | SERVINGS: 2

INGREDIENTS:

2 slices of Boar's Head No Salt Added Turkey Breast

Chopped or shredded kale

6-8 slices of walnuts

4-6 half slices of grapes

PREPARATION:

To assemble roll-ups: Place turkey on cutting board. Top with kale, walnuts, and grapes.

Starting on one side, carefully roll-up turkey until turkey has been tightly rolled. Secure roll up with a wooden pick. Repeat with remaining ingredients.

TURKEY, GREEN BELL PEPPERS, ROASTED PUMPKIN & YELLOW BELL PEPPERS

PREP: 10-15 MIN | COOK: 30-35 MIN | SERVINGS: 2

INGREDIENTS:

2 slices of Boar's Head No Salt Added Turkey Breast

2-4 cooled slices of pumpkin

4-6 yellow bell peppers, ¼ inch thick

4-6 green bell peppers, ¼ inch thick

PREPARATION:

Preheat oven to 450 degrees. Place pumpkin on parchment paper. Roast until pumpkin is tender, 30 to 35 minutes, tossing once and rotating sheets halfway through. Optional to add olive oil. 1 Tbsp

To assemble roll-ups: Place turkey on cutting board. Top with pumpkin, and bell peppers.

Starting on one side, carefully roll-up turkey until turkey has been tightly rolled. Secure roll up with a wooden pick. Repeat with remaining ingredients.

TURKEY, GREEN BELL PEPPER, TOMATO, ROMAINE & RED ONION

PREP: 10-15 MIN | COOK: N/A | SERVINGS: 2

INGREDIENTS:

2 slices of Boar's Head No Salt Added Turkey Breast

Chopped or shredded romaine

4 slices of tomato

4-6 slices of red onions, raw or roasted

4-6 slices of green bell pepper, ¼ inch thick

PREPARATION:

To assemble roll-ups: Place turkey on cutting board. Top with romaine, tomatoes, bell peppers, and onion.

Starting on one side, carefully roll-up turkey until turkey has been tightly rolled. Secure roll up with a wooden pick. Repeat with remaining ingredients.

TURKEY, GREEN, RED & YELLOW BELL PEPPERS

PREP: 5-10 MIN | COOK: N/A | SERVINGS: 2

INGREDIENTS:

2 slices of Boar's Head No Salt Added Turkey Breast

4-6 slices of red bell pepper, ¼ inch thick

4-6 slices of yellow bell pepper, ¼ inch thick

4-6 slices of green bell peppers, ¼ inch thick

PREPARATION:

To assemble roll-ups: Place turkey on cutting board. Top with bell peppers.

Starting on one side, carefully roll-up turkey until turkey has been tightly rolled. Secure roll up with a wooden pick. Repeat with remaining ingredients.

TURKEY, MANGO & RED BELL PEPPER

PREP: 5-10 MIN | COOK: N/A | SERVINGS: 2

INGREDIENTS:

2 slices of Boar's Head No Salt Added Turkey Breast

2-4 slices of mango

4-6 slices of red bell pepper, ¼ inch thick

PREPARATION:

To assemble roll-ups: Place turkey on cutting board. Top with mango and bell peppers.

Starting on one side, carefully roll-up turkey until turkey has been tightly rolled. Secure roll up with a wooden pick. Repeat with remaining ingredients.

TURKEY, NECTARINE & RED ONION

PREP: 10-15 MIN | COOK: N/A | SERVINGS: 2

INGREDIENTS:

2 slices of Boar's Head No Salt Added Turkey Breast

4-6 slices of red onion, raw or roasted

2-4 slices of nectarine

PREPARATION:

To assemble roll-ups: Place turkey on cutting board. Top with nectarine and onion.

Starting on one side, carefully roll-up turkey until turkey has been tightly rolled. Secure roll up with a wooden pick. Repeat with remaining ingredients.

TURKEY, NECTARINE, STRAWBERRY & WALNUTS

PREP: 10-15 MIN | COOK: N/A | SERVINGS: 2

INGREDIENTS:

2 slices of Boar's Head No Salt Added Turkey Breast

2-3 thin sliced strawberries

2-4 slices of nectarine

6-8 slices of walnuts

PREPARATION:

To assemble roll-ups: Place turkey on cutting board. Top with nectarines, walnuts, and strawberries.

Starting on one side, carefully roll-up turkey until turkey has been tightly rolled. Secure roll up with a wooden pick. Repeat with remaining ingredients.

TURKEY, OLIVES, ONIONS, SPAGHETTI SQUASH & TOMATOES

PREP: 10-15 MIN | COOK: N/A | SERVINGS: 2

INGREDIENTS:

2 slices of Boar's Head No Salt Added Turkey Breast

Cooled roasted spaghetti squash strands

2-4 slices onion, raw or roasted

4 slices of tomatoes

4-6 half slices of olives

PREPARATION:

Heat oven to 375 degrees. Brush the inside of each half of spaghetti squash with olive oil and sprinkle with coarse salt and freshly ground black pepper. Place cut sides up on a rimmed cookie sheet and put sheet into the oven. Bake for about 40 minutes, or until you can easily pierce the squash with a fork. Let cool for about 15 minutes, or until squash is cool enough to handle.

To assemble roll-ups: Place turkey on cutting board. Top with spaghetti squash, onions, tomatoes, and olives.

Starting on one side, carefully roll-up turkey until turkey has been tightly rolled. Secure roll up with a wooden pick. Repeat with remaining ingredients.

TURKEY, ONION, ROASTED PUMPKIN & TOMATO

PREP: 10-15 MIN | COOK: 30-35 MIN | SERVINGS: 2

INGREDIENTS:

2 slices of Boar's Head No Salt Added Turkey Breast

2-4 cooled slices of pumpkin

4-6 slices of onion, raw or roasted

4 slices of tomatoes

PREPARATION:

Preheat oven to 450 degrees. Place pumpkin on parchment paper. Roast until pumpkin is tender, 30 to 35 minutes, tossing once and rotating sheets halfway through. Optional to add olive oil. 1 Tbsp

To assemble roll-ups: Place turkey on cutting board. Top with pumpkin, onions, and tomatoes.

Starting on one side, carefully roll-up turkey until turkey has been tightly rolled. Secure roll up with a wooden pick. Repeat with remaining ingredients.

TURKEY, RED ONION, SPINACH & TOMATO

PREP: 10-15 MIN | COOK: N/A | SERVINGS: 2

INGREDIENTS:

2 slices of Boar's Head No Salt Added Turkey Breast

4 slices of tomato

4-6 slices of red onion, raw or roasted

8-10 leaves of spinach

PREPARATION:

To assemble roll-ups: Place turkey on cutting board. Top with spinach, tomato, and red onions.

Starting on one side, carefully roll-up turkey until turkey has been tightly rolled. Secure roll up with a wooden pick. Repeat with remaining ingredients.

TURKEY, ROASTED ONION, SPINACH & TOMATO

PREP: 10-15 MIN | COOK: 25-30 MIN | SERVINGS: 2

INGREDIENTS:

2 slices of Boar's Head No Salt Added Turkey Breast

4-6 slices of onion, raw or roasted

4 slices of tomato

8-10 leaves of spinach

PREPARATION:

Adjust oven rack to lowest position; heat to 400 degrees. Cut onions in half, toss with oil and a generous sprinkle of salt and pepper. Place cut side down, on a lipped cookie sheet. Roast until tender and cut surfaces are golden brown, 25 to 30 minutes.

To assemble roll-ups: Place turkey on cutting board. Top with spinach, tomato slices, and onion.

Starting on one side, carefully roll-up turkey until turkey has been tightly rolled. Secure roll up with a wooden pick. Repeat with remaining ingredients.

TURKEY, ROASTED PUMPKIN & YELLOW BELL PEPPER

PREP: 10-15 MIN | COOK: N/A | SERVINGS: 2

INGREDIENTS:

2 slices of Boar's Head No Salt Added Turkey Breast

2-4 cooled slices of pumpkin

4-6 slices of yellow bell pepper, ¼ inch thick

PREPARATION:

Preheat <u>oven</u> to 450 degrees. Place pumpkin on parchment paper. Roast until pumpkin is tender, 30 to 35 minutes, tossing once and rotating sheets halfway through. Optional to add olive oil. (1 Tbsp)

To assemble roll-ups: Place turkey on cutting board. Top with pumpkin and bell pepper.

Starting on one side, carefully roll-up turkey until turkey has been tightly rolled. Secure roll up with a wooden pick. Repeat with remaining ingredients.

TURKEY & STEAMED ASPARAGUS

PREP: 5-10 MIN | COOK: 5-10 MIN | SERVINGS: 2

INGREDIENTS:

2 slices of Boar's Head No Salt Added Turkey Breast

6-8 spears of asparagus

PREPARATION:

Wash asparagus. Cut off ends and steam until stem are cooked but still firm.

To assemble roll-ups: Place turkey on cutting board. Top with shredded lettuce, 2 tomato slices, and 1 slice of bacon cut in half.

Starting on one side, carefully roll-up turkey until turkey has been tightly rolled. Secure roll up with a wooden pick. Repeat with remaining ingredients.

FINAL THOUGHT

I hope you have enjoyed the recipes in this book. They have helped me out tremendously over the years and my hope is that they will be an asset to you on your health journey.

In closing, please note that diets come and go. The best way to maintain your health and ultimately keep the bulge off your midsection is to implement and blend a healthy food regimen into your current lifestyle.

If you are tired of yo-yo diets, starvation diets, and diets that do not work just remember this simple phrase: To thine own self be true!

If health is your chief concern and you are motivated by looking good in those skinny jeans, then get with the AOP lifestyle and you will find yourself not only in those skinny jeans but leading the healthy life you've always wanted. Remember, Health is Wealth!

Cheers to your health!

ABOUT THE AUTHOR

Frankie Roe is a mother, grandmother, author, speaker career coach, entrepreneur, and founder of Frankie Roe Exhorting Enterprises. She was born with a "go get 'em" attitude and an entrepreneurial spirit, making crafts and jewelry by age 12 and selling them door to door in her neighborhood.

Frankie's entrepreneurial spirit has grown into a full-fledged career in sales, where she has quickly ascended into management and leadership roles.

Ms. Roe is driven by a desire to see others succeed, and this shows in every aspect of her life. As a career coach, speaker, and author, she guides people to where they want to be and empowers them to be more and live a purposeful life. She loves to see clients enjoying stress-free lives and achieving professional and personal success.